Responsive

**What It
Takes To
Create
A Thriving
Organization**

Robin Peter Zander

Legal Disclaimer

On the Shoulders of Giants

I am grateful to the six people who wrote the Responsive Org manifesto, and began a movement: Adam Pisoni, Aaron Dignan, Matthew Partovi, Mike Arauz, Steve Hopkins and Alexis Gonzales-Black. They put words to a problem faced by organizations today and gave us a language to describe the challenges and tensions that have long existed in the workplace.

I would not have written this book without the friendship of Steve Hopkins, who taught me how to run an unconference, and the handful of collaborators with whom I produced my first Responsive events.

I'm indebted to the fifty-plus leaders who I've interviewed on my podcast, The Robin Zander Show, who described big ideas like *non-hierarchy* and *holacracy* in simple language and gave me hope that I could write a book to do the same.

Acknowledgements

For me, writing is always the most difficult part, and I simply would not have finished this book without help.

Shelby Vandenberg, lawyer and editor, was my first thought partner and contributor. She read and re-wrote many of the early drafts of the book. More than once Shelby talked me out of quitting and persuaded me there were people dissatisfied with their work who would find my ideas worth reading.

Ellyn Kerr, with whom I worked to produce Responsive Conference 2017, and whose insights into organizations helped inform the book's structure.

And to my editor Ann Maynard of Command+Z Content, who I'm delighted to work alongside yet again.

Most of all, though, I'm grateful to the Responsive Community. To everyone who has attended un-conferences, dinners, or the annual Responsive Conferences, I wrote this book for you. I hope it may serve as a reference guide for building your own future of work companies.

How To Use This Book

My career path has never followed a traditional route. My first job out of college was as a management consultant, with a gig as a circus performer nights and weekends. Of course, I couldn't tell the consulting company that I was in the circus, but I also couldn't admit to my fellow circus artists that I wore a suit to work. I am not content to live in such a binary world. I want to live in a world that encourages the full expression of every individual, and I am dedicated to building it. Improving the ways we work seems like a great place to start.

Responsive is a compilation of tactics and accompanying short stories about innovators on the front lines of the future of work. It is designed to be a choose-your-own-adventure exploration into how we work in the modern era, the approaches and perspectives employed by high performing organizations, and what makes those methods so effective.

While this book can be read cover to cover, I have designed it so that you can jump to those sections most interesting or relevant to you right now. Ultimately *Responsive* is intended as a reference guide as much as a road map—a resource you can return to again and again as you dive deeper into Responsive and the future of work.

A Responsive Cafe

I have a vested interest in discovering what works for myself and my small team. Throughout this book, I'll share stories about my small business, a coffee shop in San Francisco, where I work with my ten-person staff to serve coffee and avocado toast and to build community.

I founded "Robin's Cafe" in late April 2016, with no prior experience as a restaurateur but armed with a clear purpose: to foster a nascent community that I knew could exist in our corner of San Francisco. We had exactly three weeks from inception to opening day, so, unsurprisingly, our first week of operations was a mess. Attendees of a conference I had organized on site wanted to support the cafe, creating a bona fide lunch rush on our very first day.

In those early weeks, we were a team of four, often making up recipes on the spot to cover orders. I look back on those times now, after having a tough day, and realize that no matter how terrible things might seem, it will never be as chaotic and insane as those first few weeks.

We desperately needed additional staff. One day, a man named Frank quietly dropped off his resume during our usual morning rush. I was up to my elbows managing an exploding keg of cold brew. But even in the midst of a coffee emergency, it quickly became clear that Frank was professional, playful, and knowledgeable about the food service industry. I hired him, and he soon became indispensable at the cafe.

On May 20, 2016, Frank had been scheduled to open the cafe. Around 9:30 a.m., I got a call that Frank hadn't shown up. "Was he sick?" I wondered. I checked to see if he'd sent me any messages, but there were none. I called him, but it went to voicemail. A week later, I sent an email, mostly in jest, with the subject, "Are you still alive?" The staff and I just assumed that Frank became a "no call, no show," something not uncommon in the service industry. Frank's cutting contact was a simple case of job abandonment. Still, it somehow didn't seem like Frank, and I wanted to make sure he was okay. I tracked down his brother on social media and messaged him. I heard nothing for several days.

Then, out of the blue, Frank's brother called me. "I'm sorry to have to tell you this," I remember him saying, "My brother is dead. He was hit and killed by a train." In that moment of shock, while I digested what I'd just heard, Frank's brother went on: "I want you to know how happy he was to be working at Robin's Cafe."

Frank's death is a constant reminder to me of how truly transient and changeable business—and life—can be. As a small business owner in those first few weeks, I had to be resilient, not just in my response to Frank's death, but to be able to mentor and support those at our cafe and in the community who knew him. I was determined to build into the ethos of our organization this realization that circumstances can change in an instant. I wanted my team to be resilient when times got tough and grateful for the days when work felt more like play. I like to think that in some way this commitment to resilience and good humor is a small homage to Frank.

That same ethos is what has compelled me to write this book and to share just some of the ways that ground-breaking organizations and individuals are exploring human-centered work. This book is an invitation to see the value of Responsive approaches and bring them into your organization as fits your vision and culture.

Contents

1

Before Responsive

Responsive Organizations are built to learn and respond rapidly through the open flow of information; encouraging experimentation and learning on rapid cycles; and organizing as a network of employees, customers, and partners motivated by shared purpose.
– Responsive Org Manifesto

If you want to know where you're going, it's important to understand where you've been. This chapter provides a brief overview of where we've come from, reminds us of what we're building on, and points to opportunities available to us now and in the future. We'll begin with a few fundamental ways organizations and management have evolved over the last 250 years.

From Scientific Management to Employee Empowerment

While using metrics to determine job performance is now a standard practice, the concept only took root in the late 19th century, when it was introduced by Frederick Taylor (1856–1915). Scientific management, or Taylorism, is credited with improvements in industrial efficiency, particularly in the productivity of labor. In Taylor's view, scientific observation could identify how best to optimize industrial processes. He believed, for example, that management should retain all responsibility for selecting and training individuals for specific jobs, instead of allowing people to self-select into their roles.

At the 1900 Paris Exposition Universelle, Taylor unveiled part of a steel factory he was then operating in Pennsylvania. The portion of the steel mill he presented had achieved a seemingly impossible feat. During that time, a maximum of nine feet of steel length per minute of operation was the norm. Taylor's invention cut fifty feet per minute! This revolutionary 500% increase in efficiency earned Taylor a gold medal from the Paris Exposition.

Of course, what didn't get factored into Taylorism was the monotony that came from eliminating skill variety and removing employee autonomy. Scientific management often overlooked the individual.

But while Taylorism aimed for robotic efficiency, others acknowledged the human aspect of work and performance. Lillian Moller Gilbreth (1878–1972), for example, aimed to improve on Taylor's methods by introducing the new science of psychology into scientific management. Believing it was important to view employees as individuals, she insisted productivity increases could be gained by better understanding the needs and working conditions of employees. Ideas that Gilbreth first introduced more than 100 years ago, such as improved lighting, ventilation, and ergonomic equipment, continue to influence conversations about work efficiency today.

Others, like Mary Parker Follett (1868–1933), advocated for power-sharing. An American social worker, Follett believed management had a responsibility to share power with those working within the organization. She was, in part, responsible for the emergence of a win-win philosophy in business and stressed that conflict should be embraced in order to achieve greater diversity of ideas.

And, explicitly recognizing the social aspect of work, Austrian psychologist Elton Mayo (1880–1949) researched a Philadelphia textiles plant with the intention of reducing employee turnover. He concluded, as have countless companies since then, that individual performance depends on social relationships as much as the job itself.

The employee/work relationship has evolved into a complex mix of scientific management and a growing appreciation of how to organize and collaborate in ways that consider the human aspects of work. Just as employees are (hopefully) no longer considered inexhaustible resources from which to maximize productivity, so too are organizations no longer viewed as solely existing for bottom-line profit.

What Now?

Taylor, and so many other management leaders whose practices we are now reconsidering, were products of their era: they were highly efficient at managing work according to values at the time. And while bureaucracy often gets critiqued or challenged today, it must be acknowledged that no organizational design system of the past was inherently "bad." In many ways, these systems were exceptional for what they aimed to achieve.

Understanding history allows us to appreciate the strengths and weaknesses of past systems, recognize the need for change, and plan for the future. There is no right way forward, and that's the point: to be "responsive" to the specific culture, internal and external conditions of a particular organization.

The contexts within which organizations operate today are far less predictable than those of Taylor's time. Responsive organizations are designed to thrive in less predictable environments, and they do so by balancing tensions along several spectra:

- More Predictability <-> Less Predictability
- Profit <-> Purpose
- Hierarchies <-> Networks
- Controlling <-> Empowering
- Planning <-> Experimentation
- Privacy <-> Transparency

We will be examining each of these tensions in this book. We'll look at what has worked—and what hasn't—in the past and the present, and we will explore a variety of companies that are finding a balance in the areas shown above. By examining these principles, and creative approaches to them, you'll be better equipped to create positive change within your organization.

2

The Future of Work (Is Here)

Some operating principles for the Responsive organization

...as the pace of change accelerates, the challenges we face are becoming less and less predictable. Those practices that were so successful in the past are counter-productive in less predictable environments. In contrast, Responsive Organizations are designed to thrive in less predictable environments...
— Responsive Org Manifesto

The world is changing more rapidly than we have ever seen before in human history. According to 2012 estimates, members of the S&P 500 were expected on average to remain in the index for only eighteen years, compared to the sixty-one years they might have expected in 1958. The anticipated lifespan of companies has dropped dramatically over the last few decades.

We also see this in the rise of the ridesharing industry—Lyft and Uber, among others—which was enabled by the proliferation of smartphones. This new industry seized a large part of the taxi market, which previously had been considered stable, if not untouchable. Similarly, the rise of home sharing—and most notably, AirBNB—was made possible by the hyper-connectivity of the Internet Age, and disrupted the traditional hotel industry.

Another example of the changing nature of the business landscape is the 2017 acquisition of Whole Foods by Amazon.com. The day the acquisition was announced, Whole Foods stock rocketed almost 30%, while the value of competitors in the grocery business dropped precipitously. The presumption, it seems, is that disruption of the grocery industry is now inevitable.

There's a broad lesson in the emergence of ride sharing, home sharing, and the Whole Foods acquisition—which is that any organization or industry is liable to be shaken up at any moment. The goal of every company in the 21st century should be to become resilient, flexible, and have the capacity to respond to inevitable change. Industries, today, can change with unprecedented speed.

The Will to Change

Desire is the first, and probably most important, element needed for organizations and individuals to change. An organizational leader interested in changing their company will face a myriad of questions and decisions about how to initiate that change, but without first establishing the willingness to change across the organization, any future implementation will hit roadblocks.

Each organization will differ in how pervasively they want to introduce Responsive principles—and that's okay! It may not make sense to implement every facet of Responsive into your organization. As we'll discuss in the pages to come, incremental changes can lead to big impacts, while still keeping employees and customers on board. Adapting your Responsive approach to fit the needs of your organization is essential. To quote former president Barack Obama, "Change is never easy, but always possible."

Adapt to the Needs of Your Organization

One of the most exciting and intriguing challenges presented by work in the 21st century is that there is no one-size-fits-all solution. The key is to focus on the specific needs and the ecosystem within and around your organization.

What environment does your company operate within?
What factors are changing that have the most significant impact?

What aspects of your organization are most ripe for disruption?

We'll explore all of these questions and many more as we make our way through a variety of stories and examples of organizations implementing new and different ways of working.

Rethink Technology

While technology isn't the specific focus of this book, it is woven throughout. The ability to communicate near-instantaneously across the globe enables collaboration and remote work in unprecedented ways. As we consider how we organize and work together in the modern world, we can't overlook the influence of technology.

Change Structures as Needed—Even When it's Hard

We'll hear more about General Stanley McChrystal and his aide de camp Chris Fussell (Chapter 4, How We Organize), who together implemented what has come to be called a "team of teams" approach to military strategy during the Iraq War. This approach was counter-cultural to the command and control operations of the U.S. military at the time. But as Chris describes in his book *One Mission: How Leaders Build a Team of Teams*, they were trying to defeat a 21st-century threat with a 20th-century playbook. Al Qaeda terrorists were spreading propaganda using YouTube and formulating plans via Internet forums, which translated into quick action. Meanwhile, the U.S. military was hobbled by its traditional command and control decision-making processes. It took a complete rethinking of how the Navy SEALs structured their decision-making to devise a new hybrid hierarchy/network model. This model empowered the people closest to the action to make the moment-by-moment decisions necessary to meet the challenges of a new and agile enemy.

Responsive doesn't argue that change is easy, only that it can offer benefits while addressing the limitations of previous systems.

Tackle the Gaps of Legacy Practices

We'll also get to know Adam Pisoni (Chapter 4, How We Organize, and Chapter 9, Inclusion and Diversity), who co-founded Yammer, the Responsive Org movement, and is now founder and CEO of the education company Abl Schools. Abl Schools is changing how principals and administrators relate to their teachers and allocate resources. The idea is to help schools better manage their day-to-day operations to be able to achieve their educational goals.

The education system in North America is still reliant on an assembly-model way of teaching and thinking. Consider the structure of most schools: there are grades, segregated by age;

there are alarm bells which tell students when to move from one classroom to the next, and the most common form of learning is to sit passively and absorb lectured lessons.

More subtly, subjects get taught according to a linear progression. Math education in the United States, for example, moves from algebra to geometry, to advanced algebra, to precalculus, to calculus. This sequence trains students to think about math in a way that only entrenches a hierarchical, linear view of how the world works. Simply put, schools in the 21st century are still designed to produce people to work in factories.

Exciting possibilities emerge when we reinvent behemoth institutions like the U.S. education system by experimenting with new approaches that leverage technology and use innovative models of collaborating. What is necessary is the willingness to experiment.

Plan for Incremental Change

It is more efficient to navigate organizational change by utilizing small, systematic adjustments than by making large, dramatic changes. Consider a ship plotting its course. It doesn't make a lot of sense to navigate by charting a path and then checking for accuracy several days, or even months, later. Most likely the ship will end up far off course. It is more effective to estimate the desired direction and then make incremental adjustments along the way.

As Steve Hopkins, co-founder of Responsive Org and VP of Customer Success at Culture Amp, notes, organizational design "happens in the millions of micro-decisions that people make." Several stories in this book highlight how navigating by incremental changes can be highly effective. Small actions may feel ineffectual, but those steps can add up to a marked change in culture and operations.

Focus on People

One of the most exciting developments in forward-thinking companies is an emphasis on people—that is, the human experience of work. Humans are no longer seen as cogs in the machine of business. Some of this is due to shifts in bargaining leverage: it is easier than ever for employees to change jobs or create enterprises of their own. Younger generations just now entering the workforce expect positive work environments and purpose-driven companies. Organizations themselves recognize that their success increasingly calls for creating cultures and environments where their employees love to work.

As I'll describe in later chapters, Adam Pisoni is emphasizing an inclusive company culture through his efforts to build a diverse team at Abl Schools. At Culture Amp, Didier Elzinga is relinquishing traditional assumptions about compensation to improve his company Culture Amp. And the founders of Buffer are embracing salary transparency to ensure equal treatment of its employees.

3

Purpose

Today people are looking for organizations that have a purpose broader than just making money. Rather than viewing profit as the primary goal of an organization, progressive leaders see profit as a byproduct of success. They aim to do well by doing good. A clear and visionary purpose brings together stunning talent, committed shareholders, partners, and communities.
— Responsive Org Manifesto

Colleague Principles at The Morning Star Company

Doug Kirkpatrick was one of the earliest employees at The Morning Star Company. Founded in 1990, Morning Star would go on to trailblaze self-management in business. But as might be expected of any start-up, let alone one committed to innovative management, the company's early days were intense times.

Morning Star is a tomato-ingredients manufacturer based out of Sacramento, California. The agribusiness and food-processing industries are notoriously old-school, known for strict command and control structures and rigid bureaucracies. The small group of employees who initiated the Morning Star project had a six-month window to start up the first factory and had committed to beginning operations on a specified day and even at a specific hour. They were a high-performance group, and Doug describes those initial weeks as a high state of flow, with each person striving cooperatively to bring the new company into existence. The company consisted of seasoned employees, and Doug, at thirty-four, was considered quite young.

Several months before the factory opened, the owner of The Morning Star Company, Chris Rufer, called a leadership meeting. The Morning Star founder and twenty-four members of the team met on the job site. They pulled steel folding chairs into a circle, and Chris passed around a page titled "Morning Star Colleague Principles."

The sheet included just two points:

- Don't use force.
- Keep your commitments.

The group spent several hours discussing what these principles meant. Questions cropped up. What happens if you have to fire somebody? What if someone quits? In the end, no one found a reason to reject these ideas, and every person there had reasons to embrace them.

Together, the group concluded that these two points were necessary and sufficient, and they would make up the core of all human interactions at the company. Adopting these principles wouldn't change the day-to-day operations of the nascent company, but they'd have clear guideposts by which they'd proceed.

What they perhaps didn't fully process at that moment (and what Doug has spent his career implementing, first at Morning Star and now with companies all over the world) was the far-reaching ramifications of adopting those simple principles. Consider, for example, that "Don't Use Force" effectively implies:

- No one can require anyone to do anything.
- No one can unilaterally make anyone do anything.
- No one can fire anyone unilaterally.
- Each person has a voice within the company and each voice is protected; no democracy or majority rules.
- Checks and balances will be inherent.

At the time, it didn't register how profoundly that meeting, and its eventual outcomes, would impact the team, and its members individually. As Doug said, "What we did would end up being very radical—but we were so busy we didn't necessarily see it since it didn't seem immediately to impact our day-to-day lives." More than two decades later, those principles—don't use force and keep your commitments—continue to serve as the bedrock of a successful, self-managed company.

Shortly before opening, Doug and his colleagues celebrated his thirty-fourth birthday outside the same farmhouse where Chris Rufer had called that fateful leadership meeting. The company has gone on to become a model of self-management and the world's largest tomato processor, handling between 25% and 30% of U.S. tomato crops.

Purpose at DonorsChoose.org

One of the most innovative non-profits in the world today is the start-up, DonorsChoose.org. It was founded in 2000, by Charles Best, who was, at the time, a social studies teacher in the Bronx, New York. Charles and his colleagues often spent their own money on school supplies for their students and would discuss in the teachers' lunchroom what materials they wished they could afford. Charles began to envision a platform for donors to connect directly with classrooms in need, providing materials requested by teachers. With the help of his students, he built the first version of the website in his classroom and invited colleagues to post material requests.

Today, the company serves as a crowdfunding platform for kindergarten through twelfth-grade teachers in schools across the United States.

DonorsChoose.org was among the first charitable crowdfunding platforms of its kind. Among the company's many accolades, it has received the highest rating from Charity Watch every year since 2005, has been shared by Oprah Winfrey as one of her favorite things, and has raised over $500 million toward more than one million projects.

Internal Purpose

As we will explore in later chapters, generating a sense of purpose among employees is not always easy. Charles, however, says that it is one of the more manageable tasks within DonorsChoose.org. First, he and his now nearly one-hundred-person company, screen for applicants who are inherently purpose driven. His favorite question to ask potential hires is: "Who are former mentors or teachers that you are grateful for?" Potential hires who cannot readily list anyone beyond their mother do not get the job. When somebody can comfortably name six or eight, they are likely to be a good fit for the company.

DonorsChoose.org has the benefit of being a non-profit enterprise with some amount of notoriety. It is easy for employees to see the benefit they provide teachers and students across North America and thus they are regularly reminded of the impact their work has.

External Purpose

However, DonorsChoose.org does not only rely on "doing good." The company paved the way for a new kind of charitable giving by soliciting corporations to offer donations on behalf of their employees. (This has since become common practice for a variety of non-profits.) A company will buy DonorsChoose.org gift cards and distribute them to their employees. Each of those employees can then choose a specific school project to fund. The program generates positive impact in the schools, a charitable act on the part of the company, and provides the employee/donors the experience of making that positive impact.

Celebrities have taken this still further. Talk show host, Stephen Colbert, gives a DonorsChoose.org gift card to each guest who comes onto The Late Show. He has been known to say that even if there was no other benefit of them coming onto his show, at least they were able to help schoolchildren in North America.

Purpose Alone is Not Enough

Even with the emphasis on internal and external purpose, Charles Best is never complacent about growing his business. His favorite work within the company is innovating and building out the product. DonorsChoose.org is constantly experimenting. As we will explore, the company has adopted a variety of atypical approaches to growing the business (see Chapter 7, Experimentation). DonorsChoose.org also practices an unusual amount of transparency (see Chapter 8, Default to Transparency). The company shares with the public where each donated dollar goes and all of their student data, like what types of projects get the most funding, is shared via a publicly accessible dashboard.

Even for an explicitly purpose-driven company, it is important to continue to test assumptions and keep pace with the rapid rate of change. DonorsChoose.org is no ordinary non-profit and remains so by continually exploring the boundaries of a 21st-century company.

Robin's Cafe: A Purpose-Driven Eatery

I've long believed companies should exist in service to their employees. Personally, I've never lasted long working for a company that did not actively strive to fulfill a broader purpose. So when I opened Robin's Cafe, I did so with a clear intention to create a coffee shop that existed to serve its employees, who, in turn, serve a broader community.

Running a food-service business in San Francisco is hard. Low margins are compounded by a high cost of living, and the highest minimum wage in the country. Further complicating the issue, there is a local (and idiosyncratic) combative relationship between coffee shop baristas and coffee connoisseurs, with each certain the other is failing to appreciate the refinements of coffee and cafe culture.

With no prior food experience and in this challenging environment, I set out to build a thriving small business that served not just our customers or the bottom line but also my employees. Whether that is through small perks like bowling with my team at the nearby bowling alley, or one-on-one mentorship with my staff, I strive to make the cafe a gratifying experience not only for me but for them as well.

One affirmation that I'm on the right track occurred when I visited the cafe at closing to do a spot check. I asked a barista, who had been working for me about six months, how things had gone that day. He turned to me and said squarely, "Robin this is the single best job I have ever had. I've grown so much. I love it here. Thank you for providing me this opportunity." Here was someone working irregular hours, in a small cafe, serving hundreds of customers every day without guarantee of minimum hours worked or what most people would consider job security. And yet, he's had a superlative work experience. That kind of gratitude drills home for me why it's always worth it to invest in building an organization that serves the people within it.

Summary: What We Can Learn From Purpose-Driven Companies

In my study of purpose-driven companies, I've seen two key characteristics: clarity of purpose and clear agreements.

Clarity of Purpose

Successful companies are clear about what they want to accomplish and why. Patagonia is an excellent example. Patagonia was founded in 1973 by avid climber Yvon Chouinard when he and his early climbing friends wanted more straightforward access to outdoor equipment. In addition to the quality of its outdoor gear, Patagonia has been lauded for its dedication to sound environmental and small-business practices. Because the company has a clear underpinning purpose—to experience and enjoy the outdoors—the company draws like-minded individuals who can readily support its mission.

Naturally, each organization's purpose will differ. Steve Jobs created Apple with the intent of building the best personal computers and a company, in his words, jam-packed with "A players." As Apple demonstrates, an organization's purpose needn't always be a social good in the traditional sense (disrupting an industry so that consumers have a more intuitive experience with their computers is as fine a purpose as any). The important thing is that employees at all levels within a company understand and believe in why the company does what it does. A shared purpose allows employees to be clear about why they are working within an organization.

This clarity is always something an organization can help their employees attain. Didier Elzinga, the CEO of Culture Amp (see Chapter 7, Experimentation), asks a surprising question of candidates looking to join the company: "How can Culture Amp help you find your next job?" They're encouraged to brainstorm where they might be five or ten years into the future, regardless of whether Culture Amp fits into that picture. Didier is creating space for potential hires to get clear about their purpose—the real reasons why they want to join his company.

Clear Agreements
Purpose-driven companies create clear, comprehensible agreements with their employees. They do everything possible to make invisible, implicit elements of the organization visible and explicit. Valve Software is an excellent example of this. Their employee handbook, which is issued to every new employee when they join the company, outlines the radical practices that make the organization unique. For example, the handbook shows a drawing of the standard Valve company desk, which is on wheels. It encourages employees to move their desks as they self-select which projects they want to work on and find the most rewarding. Valve has clarified this expectation of employees—that they are responsible for pursuing the projects they are most excited about by literally moving their own desks.

An organization's commitment to a clear mission and clear expectations creates an army of individuals eager to fulfill that purpose on the organization's behalf.

4

How
We
Organize

In the past there were big and complex tasks that required many people working on them. The 'transaction costs' involved to get coordination between people was high, so the concept of a Manager was introduced. As the number of Managers increased, a Manager of the Managers was created... and hierarchies formed.

This resulted in order, clarity of authority, rank, and power. They reinforced a single primary connection: manager to worker, and enabled a command and control style of leadership that was terrifically successful during the industrial era.

Today, technology and connectivity has increased our ability to self-organize, collaborating more easily across internal and external organizational boundaries. It is no longer necessarily *true that coordinating through a Manager is more effective than people self-organizing. Working as a network allows us to organize with many different kinds of connections, and increased autonomy.*

— Responsive Org Manifesto

Community at Wikipedia

Wikimedia, the parent company of Wikipedia, operates in many ways as a community-based, volunteer-run organization. The company comprises about 300 employees who together manage an infrastructure accessed by half a billion users each month. Relative to almost any other company in the world, that's a massive employee to user ratio.

The majority of Wikipedia's content is generated by anonymous volunteer editors around the world who often take personal responsibility for the accuracy and up-to-dateness of Wikipedia's pages. In the words of Gayle Karen Young, Wikimedia's former Head of People and Talent, "We have no idea who these folks are—and they are the ones shaping this company." Built into the design of the company is an implicit faith in that community.

This trust has never been more evident than when Wikipedia decided to shut down the website to make a political statement. To appreciate the implications, consider that most technology companies consider downtime anathema; a company's product or software must be available to all customers at all times. In spite of this, Wikimedia's community and employees willingly chose to shut down Wikipedia for a day to advocate for net neutrality.

The Stop Online Piracy Act (SOPA) was a 2011 bill introduced into the United States House of Representatives to combat online copyright infringement. It proposed to allow copyright holders to seek court orders against websites facilitating copyright infringements. Opponents, including the Wikimedia community, rejected the sweeping powers the bill would grant to censor online activity. Wikipedia was founded to be more than just a free online encyclopedia. Gayle uses the analogy of a public park—an area for people to gather without fear of censorship or discrimination. Baked into Wikimedia's operations and mission is the concept of net neutrality, a "public park" space within the Internet.

Gayle recalls the weekend in January of 2012 that the community decided to shut down their site to protest SOPA. It was a holiday weekend, but everyone was working. As the idea of the protest shutdown gained momentum, engineers chose not to wait on leadership approval but to bring the decision to the community. Wikipedia's editorial process makes it a perfect tool for online, asynchronous voting—and the community voted to take down the website for a day. The move contributed to a tangible policy impact, and the SOPA bill died. What's interesting for our purposes here is that Wikimedia coalesced as a group of people willing to fight for a shared belief. Gayle and those she worked with during the SOPA weekend maintain a lot of pride in what they accomplished.

To remove access to a website like Wikipedia, which has more than 500 million monthly users, was a boldly countercultural move: they choose to sacrifice Wikimedia's commitment to accessibility in order to take a clear stand for the legislative foundations that would allow the company to keep that promise of a censorship-free Internet in the future. In the end, the SOPA story set the tone for the relationship between Wikimedia and its community, defined their purpose and the lengths to which they were willing to fight for it collectively, and set a precedent for future activism.

The Shape of the Organization Matters

Conway's Law states that organizations that design systems are constrained to produce designs that are "copies of the communication structures of these organizations." Simply put, the shape of an organization determines the shape of the products it creates. The ways we communicate and organize are part of what we create.

Adam Pisoni, co-founder of Yammer, recounts how he learned about Conway's law: "At Yammer, we believed in rapid product iteration. Once we realized the organizational structure was part of the product, we then had to believe in rapid organization iteration."

This insight led Adam to recognize that he and the engineering and product teams at Yammer were not just building a product; they were building a company. He began to investigate what it would mean not only to iterate on Yammer's product rapidly but also the structure of the organization itself.

In other words, he began to explore whether Yammer could become more Responsive. Adam understood that their product didn't exist in isolation. Yammer, as a communication platform for enterprise businesses, was particularly well placed to recognize the challenges of the current working world. Eventually, Adam put these thoughts into a manifesto and shared them with CEOs and C-level executives. The response was an enthusiastic affirmation of these ideas. The result of this thinking led Adam to co-found the Responsive Org movement.

A Self-Organized Community Kitchen

Three Stone Hearth, a worker-owned cooperative in Oakland, California, is a "community-supported kitchen" offering sustainably produced meals through pick-up, delivery, and a storefront location.

The company was created in 2006 by five founder/owners, who shared a vision of providing healthy food throughout the San Francisco Bay Area. Their way of working together could best be described as egalitarian. With such a small group doing all the work of building Three Stone Hearth, they were inherently self-managed and self-organizing. If one had a talent or passion for a specific area of the business, that person had the freedom to pursue it.

At the beginning, they were able to maintain and build the business without establishing clear roles. The founders all rejected management hierarchy; instead, they gathered for a meeting each week to make decisions about the company. Three Stone Hearth governance consisted of getting together and discussing issues until everyone agreed.

Initially, they met every Monday at 7 a.m. for one hour. As the business grew, meetings got longer—and more unwieldy, as they faced new pain points without simple or clear solutions. Seven years later, those weekly Monday meetings had routinely stretched until 1 p.m. (a full six hours!), with the leadership team often finding themselves going down many consecutive rabbit holes as they tackled each issue in turn.

It became clear that a new system with clear boundaries and roles was needed. The original management structure had been based on what the founders had done instinctively: consensus-building born of camaraderie. But now there was no specific protocol or framework in place to handle the growing company. Each person did the work they felt most drawn to, but the team overall lacked leadership.

Three Stone Hearth tested the system of self-organization called "Holacracy" as a possible self-governance solution to their leadership challenge. (We'll look more closely at Holacracy in the next section.) Co-founder Jessica Prentice describes how the team wrote out every activity of the business on sticky notes and then clustered them into natural groups. These naturally occurring groups would then define the functional roles at Three Stone Hearth.

Consider one of Three Stone Hearth's co-founders, Porsche Combash, who was the person everyone went to if they'd hurt themselves on the job. She didn't have a defined role but enjoyed tending cut fingers, stocking first aid supplies, and generally looked after everyone. Porsche now fills the role they call "Mother Seacole," encompassing first-aid care and supplies. Everyone in the company knows that, if you're injured, you report to Mother Seacole.

Another role is that of "Ice Man" who is in charge of the walk-in freezer. Before the position was introduced, that freezer had consistently been poorly managed, with boxes stacked to the ceiling and produce often going bad. Now, the "Ice Man" will come and tell the "Product Coach," that there is extra chicken in the freezer and that "We have to do something on the menu with chicken."

Three Stone Hearth has now grown to nineteen worker/owners and a staff of nearly fifty. The company continues to customize self-management to accommodate their growth and allow the organization to operate more freely.

Holacracy at Zappos

Alexis Gonzales-Black is a co-founder of the Responsive Org movement, and one of the people responsible for the largest ever implementation of holacracy: at Zappos, the world-famous online shoe company. Alexis describes holacracy well:

> "Holacracy is a set of rules that allows an organization to be self-organizing. Holacratic organizations operate as incredibly transparent circles, and people are free to direct their time into different projects and to pitch themselves for different projects. You could imagine every team at a company being its own tiny start-up. One of those rules, for example, is: You are free to take any action necessary to fulfill your purpose as long as it doesn't infringe on the explicit domain of somebody else."

As the idea of holacracy at Zappos gathered momentum, Alexis threw her energy behind it and went from being a member of a pilot group to one of the two people responsible for leading the entire Zappos holacracy initiative. This happened because she organically took the lead. In her words, Alexis "showing up at meetings and helped until [she] became essentially indispensable."

In the end, 100% of Alexis's work was dedicated to implementing holacracy and taking the company from "operating under the traditional management structure and executing and leading a team there, to trying to inspire and engage people to adopt something that was really uncomfortable and challenging."

But no matter how inspiring the goal of a self-managing company might be, getting there wasn't easy. Says Alexis, "We went through a lot of emotion. We quickly realized how difficult this change process was going to be, and naturally, those of us advocating for it were getting frustrated. 'Why don't people get this?' To those of us on the organizing team, holacracy was clearly so natural, emergent, organic. I couldn't fully get why others didn't feel the same way."

Far from being a loose system, holacracy involves specific protocols to determine who leads meetings and who may speak during meetings and when. As Alexis recounts, "Everyone came into the implementation of holacracy bright-eyed and bushy-tailed. But when we first tried out the format, no one knew quite what to do or how to be heard. Those leading the first couple of meetings had to keep correcting the people who wanted to speak. It was as though one day, everyone was excited about holacracy, feeling super-jazzed. And then we showed up the next day for meetings and—it was 'crickets,' no one ending up saying a word."

Imagine the absurdity of this if you were one of those in the room during those early meetings. It would feel as if someone suddenly changed all the operating rules but didn't tell you what they were.

In the years since, some of the challenges of holacracy at Zappos have been smoothed out—even while the company, and holacracy itself, have been subject to criticism. But while a Responsive approach will never eliminate all problems, having systems in place to simplify decision-making and empower people to fulfill their roles must be a step in the right direction.

An Octopus Goes to War: Hybrid Models of Organizing

In the midst of the Iraq War, the U.S. Military was facing a new challenge it couldn't seem to crack. Enemy forces had become adept at using social media and other technology to organize attacks. Quick decisions had to be made as to how to reorganize traditional military systems and processes. But with American lives, mission success, and millions of dollars of military budget at stake, no one was about to adopt a completely foreign system of organizing; something like holacracy would be too far a departure from the bureaucracy of how the U.S. military works.

It was at this time that U.S. Navy SEAL Executive Officer Chris Fussell and his cohort adopted a hybrid model blending characteristics of both hierarchy and networks, which they came to refer to as a "team of teams" approach. Rather than operating like a brain, Chris's teams would be more like an octopus.

Simplistically speaking, the human nervous system is controlled top-down, from the brain. Every behavior, thought, and emotion originates in the brain, and feedback received from the peripheral nervous system ends up back in the brain. By contrast, the octopus has a nervous system embedded throughout its body with a majority of its neurons in its tentacles. This is a crucial point; its structure allows each of an octopus's tentacles to act somewhat autonomously. If an octopus's tentacle were to become severed from the body, that tentacle could continue to operate independently, like it did when it was attached.

One of the ways the Joint Special Operations Task Force built this hybrid model was through an Operations and

Intelligence (O&I) forum—a daily ninety-minute all-hands video conference, with hundreds of people coming online from all over the globe to get on the same page about strategy and tactics over the next twenty-four-hour cycle. This large daily video conference gave the Task Force the ability to maintain an understanding of, and build continuity across, globally divided teams. The result was an approach that brought success to critical military missions and that Chris now teaches through the McChrystal Group (see Chapter 5 on Leadership).

A global company-wide video call might not be practical for every organization. And the team of teams approach is not necessarily the right hybrid for your organization.. But variables like global disbursement and distributed decision-making need to be taken into consideration by any large organization attempting to become more Responsive.

Systems (Still) Matter

When I opened Robin's Cafe, I did so with next to no preparation and without knowing a lot about the fixtures, furniture, and equipment that make a restaurant run. Over the course of our first year of operation, we were so busy building the team and serving our customers that things like equipment maintenance never got prioritized until something went wrong. I suspect this may hold true for many small businesses and even some larger organizations.

Recently, our ice machine stopped producing ice. My manager was forced to buy bags of ice from the grocery store for the cafe to be able to continue to serve iced coffee for the rest of the day. Over several hectic hours, I called friends in the industry hunting for an ice machine repairman (a niche need indeed!).

I eventually connected with a repairman and met him at the cafe late that same afternoon. Within fifteen minutes he had the ice machine up and running again. He showed me what had gone wrong and how to fix it in the future. He then proceeded to scope out all of our refrigerators. By sight, he diagnosed our soft serve machine, which had been troublesome from the start. He quickly made recommendations for a return visit on a regularly scheduled basis to maintain the ice machine and our refrigerators going forward.

In retrospect, it seems obvious to have consistent maintenance to support the equipment and infrastructure that allow Robin's Cafe to operate. But it took me a year to recognize that need and put a new system in place.

Takeaways On How We Organize

Companies can organize in a wide variety of ways. Regardless of the model your organization adopts, some vital Responsive principles are useful to consider.

There is No One-Size-Fits-All Approach

There are not hard and fast rules that classify a Responsive organization, but instead principles based on how humans naturally work together. Any change you undertake needs to make sense within the context of your organization's existing culture and according to what you're trying to achieve.

When Zappos implemented holacracy, it was a change that made sense for its particular culture. For the U.S. Navy SEALs, self-organization would have been too drastic a transformation and ineffectual for its goals. The balance you decide upon between hierarchy and a self-organizing or networked model has to be chosen within the context of your organization's identity and desired outcomes.

Consider the Changing Nature of Technology

Whether it is in the form of a 300-person company supporting half a billion monthly users or terrorists self-organizing by text message, technology is undoubtedly changing how we organize. This doesn't diminish the need for clear systems, but rather adds to the complexity of an already challenging environment.

Consider the following questions:
Where does technology overlap with your company or ecosystem?
How does changing technology open up new markets or leave your organization open to being challenged?

This issue is neither inherently good nor bad, but organizations that ignore the influence of rapidly changing technical environments do so at their own risk.

5

Leadership

Responsive leaders are a new breed, unbound by Industrial-era ways of working. These new leaders embrace the principles of creating great places to work, fostering individual development, and building resilient processes. While their approaches may differ, all the future-facing leaders I've met are curious, adaptable, and looking for the solutions that best suit their organizations today. These leaders recognize that there is no one right answer to the question, "How do we work in the 21st century?" They are willing to experiment to discover solutions that may be novel, atypical, or even antithetical to traditional techniques.

Community-Driven Leadership

When I think about the idea of emergent leadership, the founding of the Responsive Conference comes to mind. While not as glorious as some of the Navy SEAL stories told by Chris Fussell, I built on an existing community and created an event that had not existed previously.

In August of 2015, I met for coffee with Steve Hopkins, one of the co-founders of the Responsive Org movement. Over the course of our thirty-minute meeting, we found a mutual interest in cultivating the community that had formed around the Responsive Org manifesto. All of the founding members of Responsive Org had moved on to their new companies, and the community remained mostly leaderless.

Steve proposed that, as an experiment, we put on an un-conference. An un-conference is an interactive, self-organizing event where the agenda is set by the attendees. Motivated by Steve's enthusiasm, six of us sat down and fleshed out the details. For a primer on how to run your own un-conference, see the resource section at the end of this book.

The night before that first un-conference, over dinner with my co-organizers, I realized that we had energy on our side and that it could be channeled into a much larger, annual event that would bring together the worldwide Responsive community.

The next morning I announced the launch of the first annual Responsive Conference. Of course, the announcement was the easy part. What followed was a nine-month marathon of event production, speaker bookings, and ticket sales.

Although the idea of emergent leadership can seem intimidating, it develops out of small easily accomplished steps. I started out as a member of a community, came up with the idea for an annual event, tested the idea through the un-conference and other small events, and received support from the founders of Responsive Org and the community at large that allowed me to build something significant. Now a new Responsive community has taken the baton and is expanding the reach of Responsive ideas.

Different Types of Leadership

Asked to think about disruptive leaders, you might include Steve Jobs, Elon Musk, or Travis Kalanick. Each of them created companies with global reach, transforming not only entire markets but how people live their lives. Simultaneously, Steve Jobs was known for putting down people whose ideas he disliked. Travis Kalanick was removed as CEO from Uber for, among other things, his acerbic leadership. I believe that their success was in spite of these qualities, not because of them. The characteristics embodied by Responsive leaders can look far different.

Stay Humble
If you saw him walking down the street, you'd likely not

peg Adam Pisoni as the co-founder of a company that sold to Microsoft for more than a billion dollars. Adam's leadership style is very specific, direct, and clear. He asks questions like, "How much time do we have available?" and "What is the purpose of our conversation today?" and then is disciplined about respecting the time or sticking to the established purpose. Simultaneously, his pace is unhurried. Adam will take as much time to ask questions about a personal problem or small business obstacle as he will to espouse future of work philosophy.

Get Excited
Pamela Slim is excited for the future of work. The award-winning author of *Escape from Cubicle Nation* and *Body of Work*, Pam isn't afraid to take a fresh perspective on the skills required in the new world of work—from corporations to non-profits to small businesses.

Pam has decades of experience doing consulting for large companies like Hewlett-Packard, Charles Schwab, and Cisco Systems. What is striking, however, is her willingness to take on the regular and systematic re-creation of her professional goals. Having worked in both Fortune 100 corporations and for start-ups, Pam is now the founder of K'e in downtown Mesa, Arizona, where she supports small businesses through classes, networking events, and virtual programs.

When I asked Pam why she had chosen to focus on small business, she immediately enthused, "Small business is sexy!" before going on to explain that 56% of new jobs in the United States were due to small business, and that these businesses account for more than 90% of the GDP.

When I asked her why small business doesn't typically get met with the same kind of enthusiasm as Fortune 100s, she said that people just don't realize, *yet*, the opportunities and depth of learning available in running a small business. As a small business owner myself, I can attest to this breadth and depth of learning that have come through building Robin's Cafe—exceeding that of any prior business experience I've had.

Excitement is a state that can be chosen and cultivated. Pam describes how after years of enthusiastically pursuing a specific focus, she eventually loses drive—and adjusts her career accordingly. This allows her professional pursuits to be sources of excitement and joy, with a rippling out effect for those who work with her.

Lead like a Gardener

An influential leader needn't be the person at the helm or the one at the back of the proverbial battlefield giving direction to those on the front lines. A successful Responsive leader can also be one who nurtures people and creates an environment in which they can thrive.

Stanley McChrystal, retired four-star General and founder of the McChrystal Group, has often been praised for his leadership model of "leader as gardener," where the leader's primary responsibility is to nurture an environment in which growth can take place. This requires an attitude of acceptance, while establishing and maintaining clear expectations, and the emotional maturity to draw the best from one's teams. When employees trust that an organization is dedicated to their well-being, and not just extractive of their work and time, they are much more likely to give the organization their all.

How to Be a Responsive Leader

Each person must determine how they will lead, but that leadership always stems from character and values. The leadership demonstrated by Stanley McChrystal, Pam Slim, and Adam Pisoni is rooted in what they personally value. The particulars of how that leadership materializes will vary depending on the situation, but an organization can't surpass the quality of its leadership. As Chris Fussell has said of the team of teams approach, leader behavior is the essential element that allows a plan to succeed. Investing in leadership—your own and that of your teams—can only pay dividends in the long run.

6

Controlling
and
Empowering

In the past, a limited number of people held the power and understanding necessary to steer the organization and its public image. Control was forced through centralized, top-down decision-making....The higher up the pyramid you were, the more power you had. This makes sense in a world where a select few people are most likely to have the knowledge and experience necessary to make the best decisions.

Today, that is no longer the case. Circumstances and markets change rapidly as information flows faster. Now the people with the best insight and decision-making ability are often people closest to the customers, on the front line, or even "outside" the typical organizational boundaries. Rather than controlling through process and

hierarchy, you achieve better results by inspiring and empowering people at the edges to pursue the work as they see fit – strategically, structurally, and tactically.
—Responsive Org Manifesto

How Not To Join a Cult

Bob Gower had no intention of joining a sex cult. He was, however, at a low point in his life and looking for answers. He discovered the sex cult because it was located in a warehouse in the South of Market District in San Francisco, and several of his friends knew the founder.

The cult was run by a charismatic woman who drew a sharp distinction between those in her inner circle and the rest of the world. It was clear, as Bob got to know the community, that the founder was gaining notoriety and the cult was on the rise. As much as it was an exciting time to be exposed to the scene, what was even more rewarding was the fulfillment offered by cult members. Bob was welcomed with open arms, and quickly developed friendships and intimate relationships with others in the group.

Looking back, Bob says that it was obviously an unhealthy scene, but at the time it was a natural progression from friendship, to intimate relationships, to living in the cult's warehouse.

Characteristics of a Cult—or Any Poorly Run Company

The mechanisms that cults use to attract and keep members are actually used by all organizations to some degree. Cults just do things in extremes.

- Cults place a "high demand" on their members, progressively raising the bar as people move toward the inner circles of the organization.
- They allow for varying degrees of commitment and involvement, but the more members become involved within the organization, the more external communities are forbidden.
- Cults are ideologically intense and offer simplistic answers.
- They encourage conformity within the organization.
- Cults are jealous of inclusion in other organizations and actively try to shut down member's participation in alternative communities.

How It Begins

Bob's exposure began gently. He was going through a divorce and lonely. He was invited to join some workshops, which involved intimacy and community and led to intense and pleasurable experiences. There is a well-documented phenomenon called "Love Bombing," where newly indoctrinated cult members are given intense and pleasurable attention. In the case of Bob's indoctrination, this took the form of attractive women sitting on his lap, staring intensely into his eyes, and saying things like, "Oh my god! I'm so glad you're here!" It was fun and sexy and kept Bob Gower coming back for more.

Indoctrination

The next phase of indoctrination is isolation from the rest of the prospective member's community and reality. For Bob, this meant getting a lot of directives: go to workshop after workshop, attend trainings, and avoid external aspects of his life.

Cults practice "Enculturalization," the use of specific words and phrases that have precise meanings within the organization, but are less meaningful to the general public. In Bob Gower's cult, these were phrases like "Oming," "Turn On," "Charge," and "Bringing People In." The language we use impacts how we show up in the world. Language that is only meaningful to members encourages people to become a part of the organization and only communicate internally.

The Commit

In any cult, there is a moment where members are expected to commit. It's usually an emotional moment. For Bob, the commitment came when the founder spontaneous called for a thirty-person workshop.

Each person stood in front of the room and was voted on by everyone else in the group. The question, subject to voting approval by participants, was: "Is your energy Going Up or

Going Down?" A friend of Bob's stood, and everyone voted that she was on the way down, because she was in love with the man she was dating. She was pressured into breaking up with her boyfriend on the spot and renewing her commitment to the cult. It was no longer love bombing, but the threat of withdrawal–the fear of getting kicked out–that forced her deeper into the cult.

Bob was one of the last people to go up on stage. When he got up in front of the group, feeling nervous, he took the plunge. "I'm in! I'm committing. I'm quitting my job tomorrow!" He recounts expecting a party in his honor. Half an hour later Bob found himself doing dishes downstairs, with everyone ignoring him. He was asked to work harder, and sacrifice his health, safety, and income in service to the organization.

Bob moved in because he thought he was going to have a lot of sex (it was a sex cult, after all). Instead, he quickly found that the cult took up his entire life. The sense of safety was stripped away, and life became unpredictable. The founder kept all of the members in a state of uncertainty about what each day would bring. Members would be assigned new intimate partners on a regular basis, regardless of their personal relationships or preferences. Members were taught to proselytize the cult doctrine and were penalized if they failed to bring in new apostles. While he was in the cult, Bob stopped paying off his credit cards and student loans. He sold his car because he needed money. It took several years and going almost totally bankrupt, but Bob eventually found his way out of the cult. Today, as a management consultant, he has made it his life's work to help companies adopt healthy, thriving practices.

Predictability: What Good Companies Do Well

Predictability is a core attribute that makes for an effective company. Dysfunctional organizations often create unpredictability among their employees. When a company implements new systems without giving staff ample lead time or doesn't offer the training necessary to complete the desired task, this becomes another mechanism for control. This sort of unreliability is enough to make anyone a bit crazy, and, as we saw in Bob's story, can lead others to try desperately to stay in the leader's good graces. In contrast, a Responsive company establishes trust and expected behavior among its employees. When employees know what to expect and what is expected of them, they can trust the organization, each other, and do their best work.

Command and Control Military

The United States military is often used to explain command and control hierarchies. But keep in mind, the military was built to be that systematized for a good reason: it is incredibly effective for training and transporting people and equipment around the world. This system has implemented the principles set out generations before by the scientific management movement (see Chapter 1). Taylor would have envied the efficiency of such a system!

When Chris Fussell joined the fight in Iraq against Al Qaeda, it was within that hierarchical system. That system was, however, not as good at building teams that could operate efficiently in the 21st century as their new-found enemy. Al Qaeda used social media networks to spread their propaganda, quickly made use of new technology like text messages to set off bombs, and allowed fighters to operate without the direct oversight of a hierarchical leader. Thus, Chris and his colleagues quickly found themselves outflanked.

As Navy SEALS, Chris and his colleagues were trained to the highest possible levels as individuals and small tightly-knit teams. They spent years training–physically and emotionally–to handle the harshest environments in the world, coordinate among themselves, and achieve objectives. This group, was the epitome of peak performance. And yet, housed within a sprawling bureaucracy, these high-performance teams were slowed down considerably by the requirement to report back up the chain of command and receive orders before, during, and after every mission and objective.

High Performance at GE

In the twenty years that Jack Welch served as CEO of General Electric (GE), revenues increased almost fivefold—from about $27 billion to $130 billion. This impressive growth was steered by a command and control culture for which Welch would become legendary.

Welch drove this growth through efficiency that was designed to eliminate uncertainties and deviations across the company. He was known for his abrasive lectures, and personally challenging managers to emphasize his ideas. Welch also popularized forced-distribution rankings that would become common across industries. Under his leadership, GE's performance management adhered to a bell-curve ranking, where the top 20% of performers were rewarded, the middle 60% encouraged to improve—and the bottom 20% fired.

Jeff Immelt, who succeeded Welch as GE's CEO from 2001-2017, took a markedly different approach. During Immelt's tenure, the company abandoned annual performance ratings in favor of ongoing feedback. He ushered in individual and cultural improvements. Managers, who once were taught through lecture, now were offered mindfulness training and teamwork seminars. He massively trimmed the company's holdings to focus on longevity. But in his sixteen years at GE's helm, share prices also dropped more than 25%.

Comparisons between Welch's and Immelt's leadership show the strengths and weaknesses in both types of management styles. Where Welch was known to be aggressive and demanding, Immelt was seen as approachable. Welch achieved massive revenue growth and shareholder value; Immelt massively streamlined the company's holdings but also saw its stock performance drop 25% or more in a decade. On the one hand are criticisms of the competitive culture at GE under Welch's performance management approach but irrefutable recognition of correlated growth and productivity. On the other are substantial drops in GE share value but a reinvention of GE culture to be more diverse and innovative.

How should GE's success be measured based on Responsive principles? Any leadership tenure can be seen as an experiment, and GE has been an exceptional study of the balance between traditional hierarchies and more empowered ways of organizing. There are no simple truths for how GE should have been run. Doubtless both Welch and Immelt led GE in the direction they thought would serve the long term needs of the company. Nor can the rise or fall in value be attributed exclusively to their work. It will be interesting to see how GE fares under its newest CEO. Immelt's intention was to transform GE to be a more trim, agile organization able to thrive in the future of work. Immelt himself has publicly recognized that the broader results of his efforts may take years yet to materialize, but he asserts that the company is now more ready for the future.

The Balance Between Control and Empower

Command and control doesn't mean dictatorial. Jack Welch was known as aggressive and demanding, but he also encouraged bottom-up and lateral communications—not just top-down; and he is said to have sent personal notes to appreciate, inspire, or guide employees at all levels throughout the organization.

Command and control could more accurately be understood to describe the degree to which uncertainty, chaos, or flexibility are avoided when it comes to specific organizational processes. It's worth reminding here that Responsive doesn't espouse fluidity over command and control. Instead, know where along the spectrum your organization lies, identify what possibilities might be achieved by moving along the spectrum, and then experiment.

Ultimately the command—empower balance comes down to permission. As Alexis Gonzales-Black observes, "Organizations exist on a spectrum when it comes to permission. Some organizations are heavily permission-based; you can't do anything without first asking for permission. 'Can I climb this ladder? Can I sign this contract? Can I pursue this lead? Can I take this action?' On the spectrum's other end are organizations where everything is assumed to be allowed except for a few explicit things. At one end is a culture where you ask permission for things; at the other, people are encouraged to do things as long as there isn't an express rule against doing that thing."

As the stories in this chapter point out, there's no one right way. What works or doesn't work will only become clear by experimenting according to the needs of your organization.

Leading Beyond Command and Control

Be a Leader
A Responsive leader empowers their teams. Empowerment of its members is a key differentiator between cults and healthy organizations that are effectively led. Instill trust and permission in the workplace. Leaders who have a strong sense of character are better equipped to empower their teams.

Control Where Needed
Being a Responsive leader doesn't mean eschewing all control. The team of teams approach was a purposeful hybrid of hierarchy and networked team empowerment. This kind of custom approach is the best way to equip groups and organizations for success—selecting where hierarchy and control are effective, and being willing to consider and implement other alternatives in the areas where they are not. In the end, Responsive is about being fluid enough to know when, where, and how much to apply Responsive principles.

7

Experimentation

Today, plans start losing value the moment they're finished. Because we can't predict the future, time and resources devoted to planning are a less valuable investment than embracing agile methods that encourage experimentation and fuel rapid learning. The opposite of planning doesn't have to be chaos. Responsive organizations still need a long-term vision, but make progress through experimentation and iteration.
—Responsive Org Manifesto

Experiments in Catering

In my own experience, I've seen the positive and negative sides of building a business based on experimentation. The value of testing hunches or trusting employees and seeing what happens feels intuitive to me. But when it comes to business realities, bottom lines, and potential impacts on people's health and livelihoods, Responsive principles take on a rightful gravity.

On September 19, 2016, I walked into our venue for the first annual Responsive Conference unsure of whether our 300 attendees would be fed, as promised. The Robin's Cafe employees catering the conference had never worked together before and had been working day and night to prepare breakfast, lunch, coffee, and snacks for the conference attendees. It was with bated breath I waited that morning for the newly created, and as-yet untested, catering arm of Robin's Cafe to arrive.

I founded both Responsive Conference and Robin's Cafe in early 2016. As I was bouncing between these two projects in the months leading up to the first annual Responsive Conference, I kept returning to the question of how I might use the cafe to benefit our conference and vice versa. Robin's Cafe had a couple staff members who were passionate about food and excited to feed my conference goers. Catering seemed like the answer.

When I first approached these two employees about the opportunity, I was cautious, but also optimistic. We had plenty of time to organize catering at the Responsive Conference, and we could always default to hiring food trucks if things didn't work out. My employees remained eager over the weeks and months leading up to the Responsive Conference. Nonetheless, there was a near-infinite number of questions. None of us had any experience in catering, and the cafe had to continue to do business as usual in the days leading up to and during the conference.

On September 17, two days before the event, I walked into the cafe around 11:00 p.m. and found both of my employees hard at work on a new sauce for the BLT sandwiches they hoped to feed our conference attendees. While we make BLTs at Robin's Cafe, we'd never needed to produce this sauce in bulk, and they were overwhelmed.

Part of running a Responsive business is trusting the people you work with, and I had done everything possible to prepare and support my employees in whatever they needed. Eventually, though, the result was out of my control. I had been clear from the beginning that catering was a nice-to-have, and that up to a week before the event, they could decide not to cater. I had also made clear that I would be busy putting on the conference in the weeks before September 19 and would be unavailable to support them at that time.

Fortunately, they did show up that first morning, in a Prius completely packed full of food for our conference attendees. And I was told by an attendee that the BLT he ate at lunch was the single best BLT sandwich he had ever tasted.

I don't expect the cafe to cater another 300-person event offsite anytime soon. But, looking back, the ability to step away from being in control and instead trust that the people I had chosen would execute what they had committed to is an essential component of what I consider a Responsive organization.

Building a "Culture First" Company

As a technology entrepreneur, you might not expect Didier Elzinga to be an exceptional storyteller. But Didier worked on Hollywood films for thirteen years before founding Culture Amp and, in that time, he came to recognize the importance of stories, and how telling stories—to employees, investors, and customers—can fuel a successful company.

Culture Amp is a fast-growing company that prides itself on using data to drive human and company performance. As founder and CEO, Didier is driven and thoughtful about all of the things that make a technology company succeed. Culture Amp strives to be, in Didier's words, a "Culture First" organization, meaning that it prioritizes its internal culture—and only then proceeds with its mission. The company focuses on customers, business development, technology implementation, and all of the other components of a successful company—but first works to create an environment in which its employees can flourish.

Culture Amp is continuously evolving and recreating itself as a culture first company, and has adopted several practices that run counter-culturally to industry standards. For instance, Culture Amp doesn't pay its salespeople by variable compensation, which goes against standard sales doctrine. Variable compensation simply means getting paid based on how much a person sells. According to Didier, many companies believe that salespeople are a breed apart—"coin-operated," or motivated primarily by direct compensation. Having worked as a salesperson in technology and several other industries, I can attest to both this standard of practice and the assumptions about it.

What Didier discovered is that this unique classification of salespeople resulted in salespeople failing to take long-term responsibility for their newly acquired clients. Culture Amp's salespeople were handing new clients off to the customer service team, expecting that no further involvement was needed on their part. When Didier realized that clients were being mishandled, and noticed the lack of communication between sales and customer service teams, he decided to obliterate variable compensation. Contrary to dampening motivation, the company was able to foster a stronger, more cohesive sales and customer service team, collectively committed to serving the long-term needs of the clients.

New Ways to Raise Charitable Donations

DonorsChoose.org regularly adjusts their core product, online donations solicited for classrooms (see Chapter 3). This might seem strange for a charity, to be testing and retesting their "products," because after all, isn't their product charitable donations? But Charles Best has relentlessly experimented to find out what motivates donors to give more in order to increase donations.

Charles started DonorsChoose.org in his classroom, when he was a social studies teacher. He funded the first ten projects himself as an anonymous donor to persuade his fellow teachers at his school that they could raise funds via the website (and convince them that donors were eagerly waiting to fund projects). With his students help, he also conducted a letter-writing campaign and solicited donations from his alma mater's alumni all over the United States.

Charles has been incredibly resourceful in reaching out to celebrities and personalities who've helped to further the DonorsChoose.org mission. Through a random phone call, Charles reached Craig Newman (founder of Craigslist), who then mentioned DonorsChoose.org on Stephen Colbert's The Colbert Report. This led to Stephen Colbert interviewing Charles. Through similar outreach, DonorsChoose.org has been listed as one of Oprah Winfrey's favorite things.

To assure donors that their money is being used honestly, money is never given directly to the classrooms, but rather DonorsChoose.org purchases and ships the supplies needed. Donors also receive personal thank you notes written by students who have been impacted by their donations.

Through their experimentation, Charles and his team have discovered several surprising things about donors. Such as, donors enjoy sponsoring classrooms in the donor's hometown. Or that people are more likely to donate toward hurricane relief if the name of the hurricane shares the initials of the donor's first name. Similarly, donors have a propensity to sponsor teacher's classrooms if they have in common the teacher's last name. Testing assumptions and experimenting with new methods are hallmarks of any Responsive company.

Remote Work

Carolyn Kopprasch joined the social media company Buffer in 2012 doing entry-level customer service. She describes feeling supported by Buffer co-founders Joel Gascoigne and Leo Widrich—even during the interview process. For instance, Joel and Leo realized that she would need to take a day off from her current job to interview, so they offered to interview her on a Saturday instead. At the time, the co-founders were working remotely from Tel Aviv, Israel, and discovered only minutes before their scheduled interview with Carolyn that their office had been locked for the weekend. Instead of postponing the discussion, they interviewed Carolyn over Skype from the street outside their office. A bit disorganized, perhaps, but their willingness to interview Carolyn despite unusual circumstances conveyed their sincerity.

Today Buffer is an entirely remote company, with employees working from around the world, but but when Carolyn joined the employees still worked in a traditional, brick and mortar office. The decision to go remote came gradually when the team realized that it didn't make sense for everyone working for the company to move to the San Francisco Bay Area.

They realized that both real estate and talented employees in the San Francisco Bay Area are very expensive. Instead of hiring people only in the region, what if they could hire anyone in the entire English-speaking world? Joel and Leo had previously had the opportunity to travel the world. They wanted their employees to have similar freedom.

Carolyn acknowledges that this approach involves tactical considerations. Having mostly remote teams can be logistically tricky and less efficient. With people calling into meetings from all over the world, the company had to take into consideration many different time zones in order to find a convenient time to meet. The Buffer team had to learn to wait twenty-four hours on important decisions to ensure input from all relevant people across the globe.

For employees, there were sacrifices and benefits to the freedom to work remotely. During a stay in Venice, Italy, Carolyn found herself facing regularly scheduled Buffer meetings at 10 p.m. local time. This meant going to bed late—but also having the freedom of luxurious mornings. For Carolyn, and many at Buffer, the benefits of being able to work from whatever country and continent they desire far outweighs any costs.

How to Experiment

Experimentation is at the heart of any Responsive organization. The goal is to react quickly with the best information at hand, and then respond to feedback, whether it be from clients, the market or employees. The following three components are needed before companies can experiment successfully.

Trust

A vital component of any organization that wants to experiment is trust in the people actually doing the work. There was a point in catering the first annual Responsive Conference where the outcome was simply out of my control and I had to trust the people to whom I had given authority. In Buffer's experiments with remote work, there was a willingness to trust that their employees would be productive outside of a traditional office setting. Had things gone poorly, they could always have moved back to a single location.

Culture

Culture is the second principle which makes a successful experimental company. General Electric couldn't have embarked on the changes former CEO Jeff Immelt ushered in without a willingness to experiment with new visions, plans, and actions (see Chapter 6). While opinions of success vary, depending on whether we're considering shareholder value or improved culture, GE is now a more agile company with a more human-focused culture than it had before.

Similarly, at Culture Amp, it took Didier Elzinga's thoughtfulness and a company focused on the well-being of people, to leave behind a model of compensation that did not suit the needs of that organization.

Incremental Change

Finally, incremental change can be used to ease the process of implementing Responsive principles. Incremental change can minimize losses and maximize learning from "failed" experiments and allow successful trials to be quickly built upon, scaled, or improved further. This doesn't mean all Responsive change must be small (as we'll see in the next chapter), but it is important to factor in the gains afforded by small cumulative adaptations.

8

Default
to
Transparency

In the past, information was the currency of power: hard to come by and hard to spread... Today, we have access to so much information that it's become impossible to predict which information might be useful or who might use that information in a productive way. In this world of abundant information and connectedness the potential benefits of trusting people who share the organization's purpose to act on information as they see fit often, outweighs the potential risks of open information being used in counterproductive ways.

— Responsive Org Manifesto

Experiments with Transparency

There are no universal rules about transparency. In exploring the implementation of Responsive principles in any given organization, there will reasonably be a pendulum swing between more-traditional and less-traditional methods. Joel Gascoigne, CEO of social media company Buffer, built his company to experiment with the oscillations of the pendulum. He is unafraid to test out hypotheses and explore new ideas; some won't work, and some lead to lasting changes within the company.One of these "lasting experiments" was with transparency. Buffer decided to make all of its salary information public.

"The Day My Salary Went Public"

In November 2012, Colin Ross discovered Buffer through a jobs board. He was struck by the company's culture and he particularly appreciated that the CEO shared Buffer's internal journey publicly, which communicated an authenticity that attracted Colin. However, he was living outside of London, and Buffer was only hiring in San Francisco at the time. So Colin gave the notion little further thought, though he did continue to keep track of the company.

In January 2014, Buffer started hiring remote workers. Without a lot of expectation, Colin submitted his resume alongside a sprawling cover letter, which opened with, "You probably have many vastly more qualified candidates than me." A month later Colin was an employee, working remotely from his hometown, outside of London, and, he remains an employee almost five years later. He has built relationships with people from all over the world and appreciates the quality of people he works alongside.

The day Buffer made its salaries public was memorable for Colin, not because of any personal impact but because of the outpouring of reactions from the public. Colin, a relatively private person, felt that he was being paid a good salary—not too much, not too little. The company had already shared salaries internally for several months, but the founders were admittedly concerned about how the public would react.

They needn't have worried, though; the public response was one of awe. In comments on Buffer's blog post, on Twitter, and in email correspondence, people worldwide were appreciative of Buffer's transparency. One person emailed, "I know more [about] the internals of Buffer than I do about my own company."

Colin explains that Buffer wasn't sharing salaries to show off, to get more applicants, or drive people to use Buffer—though all of these did occur as a result. Buffer decided to share this data, somewhat naively, because it felt like the right thing to do. It felt in line with the ethos of the company and was something overall that everyone wanted. Colin says he has only positive feelings about being part of a culture so open about itself and its process. And while Colin may not have recognized it, that initial announcement about Buffer salaries was a watershed moment in a more global movement toward transparency.

Salary as Conversation Starter

Hailley Griffis is a communication specialist at Buffer. As such, it is perhaps unsurprising that conversations about Buffer's salary transparency, and especially her own salary, have resulted in fascinating, vulnerable, and often hilarious, discussions about money.

While attending a technology conference, a fellow attendee asked about Buffer's "default to openness" policy. Over the course of several minutes, he mustered the courage to ask her about her salary. Since it was posted online anyway, it was a perhaps a more expected question than it would have been otherwise. When Hailley shared her salary, she got several mixed reactions. One onlooker said, "You make way more than me!", while the person who'd asked the question said, "You make way less than you should."

Both of these attendees eventually shared their salaries, as well. The conversation, and Buffer's policy, had created an openness and camaraderie that rarely occurs around money. The conversation ended with one of the attendees exclaiming, "You two are the only people in the world who know my salary!"

Hailley now actively brings up money and earnings in social contexts as an experiment to see whether she can cultivate the same kind of camaraderie she experienced that day. This highlights the rippling effects well beyond a company that transparency can create.

Everything Transparent

At Buffer, salaries aren't the only thing out in the open. Nearly everything is transparent. Of course, not everyone reads everything, but virtually all information within the company is made available internally. Buffer leadership realized early on that a rapidly growing globally distributed team would be more effective if they were not protective with their information.

This isn't to say there haven't been downsides. For example, in the company's early days, if an email were read by, say, one person to whom it was addressed and three CC'd, and if that email took twenty minutes for each to read and respond to, that would account for an hour and twenty minutes of human-hours. Theoretically, if that same email were now sent to seventy people, that could consume almost twenty-four hours of time spent on a single email. As Carolyn Kopprasch (see Chapter 7), says, "We spend a lot more of our time than is fully necessary reading email," which slows things down.

...Or Maybe Not Everything

Even though there's currently a push towards transparency, sometimes privacy is also necessary. For example, DonorsChoose.org (see Chapter 7), engages in a variety of transparent practices. They share real-time statistics about the impact of donations on specific classrooms. They have a dashboard compiling data on the outcomes of all contributions, projects funded, and students reached. However, they are also highly sensitive to the privacy needs of their platform, given that the population they ultimately serve is schoolchildren. For this reason, the organization has strict policies in place to protect privacy.

In providing a forum for teachers to share their classroom's needs, the organization has expressly required that teachers do so without disclosing children's personal information. In posting photos of their classroom needs, for instance, teachers cannot use pictures that show a child's face as more than one-fifth of the entirety of the image because more could reveal the identity of that child. All data on the DonorsChoose.org data dashboard is anonymized for the same reason.

This example highlights the need to balance transparency with the specific privacy needs of one's own company and culture. The move towards transparency cannot overstep the privacy needs of select parties. As always, there is no single ideal solution, and each organization or team needs to identify a balance that works best for them. What Responsive encourages is the openness to experiment with new ways that may seem counterintuitive.

Lessons in Transparency

Just Try It On

Not every company is going to immediately experiment with the transparency of normally private data. The specifics of a particular industry matter, and regulated industries may not always have a choice about what they are obliged or forbidden to share.

But it is a common trend for Responsive organizations to at least experiment with the openness of information. Information is a critical factor in empowering all people within the company to do their jobs well. Transparency can change mindsets, broaden people's perspectives, and create positive effects on culture. If making information public is not an option, consider making more information available internally.

Leverage Technology

Technology is both a driver of growth and a challenge for Responsive companies. Technology is disrupting entire industries and changing consumer patterns and communication possibilities globally. No edict says companies must be fully transparent, and yet the world is increasingly connected. Data and knowledge that are guarded heavily may be leaked or accidentally distributed despite best efforts and it can be useful to recognize and adapt to this fact. Organizations willing to proactively explore how technology and data openness can create benefits are a step ahead of those more guarded and reluctant to embrace the realities of technology progression.

9

Inclusion
and
Diversity

You might think that disruptive, forward thinking, companies like Uber and Google would have addressed inclusion and diversity. But Uber has faced a slew of recent challenges: including well-documented allegations of sexual misconduct throughout the company. Meanwhile, Google, is facing Department of Labor allegations about extreme gender pay disparities. Outside of technology, too, this problem is pervasive. More cases of sexual harassment, in fields ranging from journalism to government, are becoming public with increasing regularity.

Diversity and inclusion issues range well beyond gender and include discrimination related to race, religion and disability to name a few. Companies need to be open to listening to employee concerns about inclusion, and fostering environments that encourage dissenting viewpoints. Organizations should strive to create environments in which people can thrive.

Diversity and inclusion are complex concepts, and a full discussion of their impacts exceeds the scope of this book. What's relevant for Responsive organizations is that diversity of opinions can create higher-performing teams, and that diverse populations continue to experience discrimination and exclusion.

Discomfort and Psychological Safety

A Responsive company is one that allows its employees to show up as themselves, and strives to enable them to express themselves—even those parts that we tend to keep hidden.

Fostering psychological safety does not mean creating a space that is without challenge. Humans can grow and learn through adversity, and most successful companies have succeeded as a result of their efforts in territory that is difficult to address. Before a series of controversies at Uber culminated with CEO Travis Kalanick stepping down as CEO, the company was lauded for its hyper-aggressive growth. That kind of rapid growth is inherently challenging and cannot be achieved in an environment that is intrinsically sheltered and protected. There is a balance between psychological safety and the discomfort that is necessary for growth.

The answer, as with most Responsive principles, lies in a unique balance that must be struck by each individual and organization, based on their unique needs. In this chapter, I'll present stories of individuals who see diversity and inclusion through a hopeful lens. These are people who have taken action toward addressing diversity and inclusion in new and exciting ways.

What's Your Exclusion Story?

Aubrey Blanche is the Global Head of Diversity and Inclusion at the technology company Atlassian. According to Aubrey, "Everyone has an exclusion story." In our first conversation, Aubrey asked me about a time that I had felt excluded. She credits this exercise to Damien Hooper-Campbel, who regularly teaches its use. It goes as follows:

1. Think of a time when you felt excluded.
2. Tell it to the person next to you.
3. Think of a time when you felt included.
4. Share it, likewise.

The purpose of the exercise is to de-stigmatize both the feelings of inclusion and exclusion. By recognizing that everyone experiences both, a conversation about diversity and inclusion becomes much more beneficial.

Aubrey's journey began at Stanford University, where she was pursuing a Ph.D. in the democratization of military strategy. If that sounds like a mouthful, it is, but it paved the way for the work she has gone on to do: building out an inclusive strategy for a global company. It was upon leaving Stanford and joining a small technology company in business development that Aubrey first realized her uniqueness. She looked around at the team and realized there were a total of two Latino people, including herself, and very few female engineers. Aubrey genuinely could not describe a moment when anyone did something negative or where she felt purposefully left out. It was instead, the realization that, that there were so few people like herself that started her work in inclusion.

Aubrey realized that the lack of diversity in her company was a solvable problem. The issue was not the specifics of her organization—or any company—but that there were inadequate systems in place to help diverse employees feel included.

She says that people make the principles of inclusion harder than they need to be. We assume that an inclusive company culture has to be perfect to be successful. Aubrey argues, instead, that companies and individuals should not strive for perfection but aim to have a positive impact. The question we should be asking is "Are people within this community positively impacted by our efforts?" It just takes the willingness to learn and adjust.

Aubrey encourages taking small steps toward building more inclusive workplaces. She adds that "The majority of the discourse is angry shouting." Instead, when we adopt the belief that each person is trying their best, we foster much more productive conversation. She frequently cites the Mark Twain quote that "continuous progress is better than delayed perfection." Under her guidance, the company has implemented gender-neutral bathrooms. What's exceptional is that this change did not come about by Aubrey's directive, but rather the signs were installed at the initiative of the employees responsible for maintaining the building.

At Atlassian, Aubrey strives to foster empathy and understanding. She says: "If you are trying and doing your best, you get a cookie. I'm a proponent of ally cookies and high-fives." Whereas most companies emphasize big diversity happy hours and diverse Employee Resource Groups, Aubrey focuses on small, achievable, measurable outcomes. She encourages employees at Atlassian to explore what they can do in their day-to-day job to make the workplace a little bit better all the time.

A Diverse Founding Team

Adam Pisoni, who we've gotten to know throughout this book (see Chapter 4), has tried some very usual approaches to diversity as the founder of Abl Schools, an educational platform striving to change the education system in the United States (see Chapter 2).

Abl is trying to serve the needs of a diverse population—kindergarten through 12th grade schools across the U.S.— and as such is benefited by having a diverse company and culture. Especially in Silicon Valley, where Abl is headquartered, technology start-ups are not known for being diverse. The founders and early employees of such companies are frequently straight, white men.

It was into this context, that Adam set out to build a diverse founding team. In an article called "In Defense of Diverse Founding Teams," Adam writes:

> "If your founding team is homogenous, it will likely develop a narrow culture which is well suited for that narrow group of people. That culture won't be as self-aware of the lack of inclusion in the culture, but it will feel inclusive for everyone within the tight knit founding team. As new employees with different backgrounds join, they will be more likely to reject or be rejected from the culture than to add to it. While you may be celebrating how strong a culture and tight a team you have, you may also be unaware of the ways you're actually reminding new employee that they don't belong."

While there is a lot of conversation about fostering an inclusive company culture, very few companies have an equal gender split in employees, and even fewer have women or other underrepresented groups at the highest levels of leadership. Adam explains that teams of straight white men can produce great companies, but he argues: "I believe diverse founding teams can produce better outcomes. A team of white men can come up with good ideas. But I believe a diverse team can come up with better ones."

With this belief, and within a relatively non-diverse ecosystem in Silicon Valley, Adam has set out to build a diverse team at Abl. This was an explicit criteria when he raised funding from investors. In conversations with investors, Adam made clear that building diversity into his core team at Abl would take more time, but was a requirement for the success of his company. He also had to overcome the limitations of his own network. As a white man living in Silicon Valley, he put in extra effort to get to know communities in which he hadn't previously been involved.

Adam has been remarkably open about the challenges of building a diverse founding team, but has made it a core priority of his growing company to hire high caliber and also diverse candidates. This has required a lot of perseverance, and unusual approaches in hiring, but the determination Adam has demonstrated at Abl Schools is an example of what can be done in any number of fields by founders just starting out.

Diversity Debt

Didier Elzinga, CEO of Culture Amp (see Chapter 7), was the first person I heard using the phrase "diversity debt." Didier describes diversity debt by likening it to the more commonly understood technical debt, where a company created a software product with poor quality code, preferring rapid execution over long-term, more laborious software development. The problem with technical debt is that it builds up over time, and must eventually be "paid off" in the form of lengthier development to improve the poorly written software. Similarly, diversity debt, as Didier coined the term, is the cost accrued by an organization when it is made up mainly of the same sort of people.

The four co-founders of Culture Amp are all straight, white, technologically savvy men. Culture Amp believes that a company made up of a diversity of perspectives is more likely to be a well-rounded organization, better able to serve a diverse audience. Unfortunately, because of hiring needs, other factors like experience or specialized skill sets often trump diversity, and thus, diversity debt accrues. Didier's willingness to acknowledge and take responsibility for the lack of diversity in his founding team, and how that has trickled out across the entire company, is laudable. I look forward to watching how Didier and Culture Amp leadership strive to resolve this diversity debt over the coming years.

Create Trust

Carolyn Kopprasch was a young employee when she first joined Buffer, and like many women, she did not negotiate her salary in starting her new job. She admits to being aware that there were probably male employees–at Buffer or elsewhere–who were doing the same work for significantly higher pay.

For Carolyn, Buffer's move to salary-transparency (see Chapter 8) was life-changing. It was this transparency within Buffer that solidified her faith in the company and in co-founders Joel Gascoigne and Leo Widrich. Here was irrefutable proof that they were committed to equal pay across gender. Carolyn says that making salaries transparent removed any doubt in the ethics of the company.

Carolyn says that she could never go back to working for a company without knowing that the organization was unequivocally dedicated to gender pay equality. As a professional, and as a woman, Carolyn feels valued by Buffer. This has instilled in Carolyn tremendous loyalty to the company.

What Does it Mean to Include Diversity?

Ultimately the value of diversity is a wider range of perspectives and ideas, and inclusion can't happen without psychological safety—where people feel invited to "bring their whole selves" to work. Here are my takes on a Responsive approach to diversity and inclusion.

Emphasize the "I"

Inclusion isn't something that a few leaders dispense to the rest of the organization. It's something baked into an organization's culture—and can't be faked. Diverse representation means nothing if individuals feel only nominally included. But more than this, the many benefits of diversity—improved performance, innovation, creativity—are accessed when individuals, regardless of ethnicity, age, job title, etc., feel empowered and free to share ideas and suggest improvements. If there is one thing that most characterizes the Responsive workplace, it is the recognition that organizations are primarily human first—everything is achieved by humans working together. An inclusive team will bring out the best in everyone.

Make it Personal

To repeat Aubrey Blanche, everyone has an exclusion story. Try the exercise and describe to a colleague an experience of exclusion, and another of inclusion. By accessing the personal experiences of people within your organization, you will be able to foster diversity and inclusion champions. Embrace the fact that the people in your organization are *human*.

10

Where To
From Here?

I'll end this book with some of the principles we have seen emerge throughout. I hope that these principles serve as guideposts for you as you embark on creating and building Responsiveness within your own organization.

Adapt to the Needs of Your Organization

To tackle 21st-century challenges organizations may need to structure themselves quite differently than they have historically.

Throughout this book, we have seen a wide variety of examples of Responsive principles in practice. A common theme is that there is no one-size-fits-all solution to how we structure the organizations of today. Instead, each of us must find a level of comfort with the particular Responsive systems and processes that support our needs. If an organization's leaders can be honest with themselves about current realities—what is working and what isn't—they may find that to remain adaptable requires changes to their organizational structure.

A resilient organization adapts itself, constantly, to the ecosystem within which it exists. The era of Taylor's principles of scientific management is over; but instead of disregarding Taylorism or any models for organizing, a Responsive organization keeps in mind those ideas without losing sight of the new demands placed upon organizations today.

It may be that a traditional management hierarchy serves the needs of your organization—or at least parts of it. There is nothing inherently wrong with a more traditional management structure. Or it may be that your company is better suited to entirely non-hierarchical management; organizations today do not fundamentally need a boss to succeed—if indeed they ever did. I am not arguing that you should do away with your current structure and replace it any specific system. For many companies, it may be that a customized hybrid model will be most useful. As Stanley McChrystal and Chris Fussell found amidst the Iraq War, many of these principles can be customized to suit the needs of a specific challenge. One just needs to be willing to intelligently analyze what will lead to effective outcomes, be open-minded enough to consider new possibilities, and be bold enough to implement those changes.

Learn what systems and practices best suit you, your colleagues, and the needs of your organization. What is certain is that how we organize in the 21st century will continue to be a puzzle and a challenge that each organization must solve for itself.

Focus on People

Responsive organizations create meaningful work environments. Profits and processes still matter—and people, purpose, and passion must be factored in.

We have seen throughout this book that the most successful organizations focus on people. Whether that is through moving away from strict profit motives, the willingness to experiment, or the exploration of transparency, Responsive companies recognize the need to build organizations in service to their people. At The Morning Star Company, we saw how its Colleague Principles enabled employees to have a more definitive purpose at work. At Culture Amp, we saw how changing standard pay structure led to a more cohesive team. At Buffer, we learned how an employee's trust in her company was deepened by their default to salary transparency.

Each of these companies, and so many more like them, are experimenting with how to enable their employees, managers, and leaders to be "more human" at work. More people around the world want to work for human-centered organization, fewer are willing to tolerate employment solely for a paycheck, and this trend will only continue.

Of course, there are clear financial motives for ensuring that employees are happy and well-cared-for. The cost of recruiting alone, and the savings implied by high retention, impact an organization's ability to survive or thrive. But well beyond financial motives, in the 21st century, organizations are increasingly human-centered. Organizations that find ways to serve the needs of the people who work within them are the ones that will thrive.

Adapt Technology

Technology advances can give Responsive organizations a competitive edge and outstrip bureaucratic companies that fail to adapt.

Although Robin's Cafe, and even Three Stone Hearth, operate similarly to how restaurants have been run for centuries, many of the examples we've seen through this book are driven by the development of technology. The pace of technological change is disrupting industries, changing our assumptions of work, and allowing explorations that were previously impossible. The very nature of Wikimedia and the global reach of the company permitted it to have an outsized impact on the political stage. Without the hyper-connectivity and public accessibility that are core to that organization's philosophy, those results would not have been possible. Similarly, DonorsChoose.org has reshaped the philanthropic landscape. While donating to charity is not a novel concept, the way in which Charles Best utilized technology is an example of how Responsive principles can be applied.

Technology is impacting industries in ways we cannot predict. Leverage the changes in communication, connectivity, transparency, location independence, and rapid iteration made possible by our increasingly technologically connected world.

Embrace Incremental Change

One final tactic that every Responsive organization applies is incremental change. Recognize the value of cumulative, small, incremental changes, as people and processes within your company adapt. Whether implementing a new system of management or entering a new market for your business, focus in on small changes. Do not roll out broad sweeping changes without first testing them in a more modest context. Be willing to experiment. Get feedback from employees, leaders, and stakeholders, and make corrections as you go.

The process of focusing on incremental changes will, in the

long run, save time and effort and allow your organization to adapt sustainably.

Concluding Remarks

This book was inspired by the dozens of stories which forward-thinking leaders shared with me, through my podcast, and as a result of curating the annual Responsive Conference and other events. It has been a privilege to hear their stories, and I am grateful for their willingness to vulnerably share what has worked (and what hasn't) so that we can learn from their triumphs and mistakes. These people are renegades, pushing some of the most important boundaries in the modern working world. It is up to us to keep pace. I wish you, and your organization, a mixed blessing: Never stop learning.

Resources

Get Involved

Attend An Event

I host the Responsive Conference, un-conferences, and many other public and company-specific gatherings throughout the year. To learn more, visit http://www.ResponsiveConference.com.

Join The Newsletter

We send out a monthly email with upcoming events, recommended reading, and more. Join the newsletter via the website http://www.ResponsiveConference.com.

Run Your Own Un-Conference

For a tutorial on how to run your own un-conference, visit http://www.RobinPZander.com/unconference.

Work With Us

I run the organization design agency Spring Space. If you are looking to implement some of the principles described, I would love to help. To learn more, visit http://SpringSpace.org.

Read the Responsive Org Manifesto

The Responsive Org Manifesto can be found at http://www.Responsive.org/manifesto.

People

For more about the individuals described in this book, and to hear in-depth interviews, listen to my podcast, the Robin Zander Show, which can be found at http://www.RobinZanderShow.com.

Episode 34: Steve Hopkins – Coffee Connoisseur, Yammer, Culture Amp and Building Responsive Organizations

Episode 35: Adam Pisoni on Founding Yammer, Responsive Org, Abl

Episode 37: How Not to Join a Cult with Bob Gower

Episode 38: Joel Gascoigne, Buffer CEO interview at 2016 Responsive Conference

Episode 39: Alexis Gonzales-Black: Zappos, Holacracy, and How We Work in the 21st Century

Episode 41: Wikipedia, Culture and Poetry with Gayle Karen Young

Episode 42: Doug Kirkpatrick on The Morning Star Company and Building Self-Managed Organizations

Episode 43: Chris Fussell: Former Navy SEAL shares how leaders build a Team of Teams

Episode 47: Didier Elzinga on storytelling, leadership and building Culture Amp

Episode 49: Pam Slim on Capoeira, Building a Body of Work, and the Value of Small Business

Episode 50: How Charles Best Created DonorsChoose.org – A New Kind of Non-Profit

Featured Companies

Abl Schools

AirBNB

Apple

Atlassian

Buffer

Culture Amp

DonorsChoose.org

General Electric

Lyft

McChrystal Group

Robin's Cafe

The Morning Star Company

Three Stone Hearth

Uber

Wikimedia

Yammer

Zappos

More by Robin Zander

Visit Robin's Cafe in San Francisco or online at
http://www.robinscafesf.com

Join Robin's newsletter for weekly updates at
http://robinpzander.com/newsletter

How to Do a Handstand: How to Learn a Fearless
Handstand in 20 Days or Less

The Accelerated Learner: Acquire New Skills, Master Fear,
and Stay Ahead of the Curve

Made in the USA
Monee, IL
03 September 2024